Poems for all Seasons
By
Suneel Rajpal

Poems for all Seasons

Inspired by the Best Teacher-Life

Suneel Rajpal

Copyright © 2008 , Suneel Rajpal

ALL RIGHTS RESERVED.

No Part of this work covered by the copyright hereon may be reproduced or used in any form or by any means graphic, electronic or mechanical, including photocopying, recording, taping, Web distribution or information storage and retrieval systems without written permission of the publisher.

To apply for permission to use material from this text or product contact us at suneelrajpal@yahoo.com

*Dedicated to those who loved and lost,
And to those who loved and found
Rather than never have loved at all*

The Journey

I boarded the train alone yesterday
It was vacant and I could work or play

I looked at the green fields outside
To quench all the thirst inside

The train stopped at many a station
Important was the journey not the destination

Many passengers shared the journey, call it fate
Parents, children, spouses, friends and soul-mate

All took a part of me, and shared my space
Beautiful moments disappeared without a trace

The essence was that we were all just passengers
Each to their destination, we were just messengers

The moments apart were like going through a tunnel
Darkness on all sides and fears went in a funnel

Finally at the end there was a white light
Where we eventually merge with His might

The Rose

I once saw a rose long ago
It was fresh, bright and yellow
I thought it was divine
I wish it would be mine

The rose was not in my garden
The thought made my feelings harden
The flower was very sad
When we met we were glad

The flower would smile with glee
With the thought of being set free
It wanted to have a life of its own
Free from the gardener and the moan

A strong breeze came one day
It took the flower far away
I went by her lane
Her absence caused me pain

In my life I saw many flowers
I still couldn't forget the many hours
Of joy I had seeing my first love
Pure as the whitest dove

Aeons later I saw her again
She had lost some petals but still the same
My heart began to pound
I only lost her to be found

She smiled again and with her glow
Covering her scars so that they wouldn't show
One look at each other and we knew
We were so alike and that was true

Spending our lives only watering others dreams
Was the cause of the problem it seems
Just holding each other once again
Rejunevated us from all the pain

She wondered if this was love
I told her by the skies above
To me she was the same flower
Who only had happiness to shower

The Time with the Rose

You don't know how good it was for my soul
You made me feel like a person that was whole

I know about the things in the past
I know that the hurt will last

But alas my precious dear
You have nothing to fear

I will give you all the space that you need
Deep inside I know that you will return indeed

For I too have also cared for you
I won't be hurt no matter what you do

Relations

She is not my mother
But she does love and care

I am not her brother
But I want to protect and share

She is not my sister
But her thoughts and teasing are so dear

I am not her father
But I want the best for her, that's clear

What binds the two of us is a strange relation
Built out of love and compassion

The greatest thing in Life is just to be loved indeed
Enjoy every moment and that's all we need

The Restless Sea

The oceans have a mighty roar
They break their energy before touching shore

The waves crash into the rocks
It is a pleasure to watch that from the dock

My mind is like the restless sea
It causes my head to have so much energy

When a loving hand touches my head
It soothes me feel like a child on a rocking bed

When I receive warmth from my soul mate
I can crash into any reef, no matter how great

That is why I am at peace in the sea
She rocks me with the waves like her baby

She will always put me ashore
Even though I want to rock some more

A better calm I will never see
Than with my mistress-the restless sea

The Ocean

The Ocean was deep and blue
The perfect place for me and you

We could wade in the water until it got too deep
And then catch a wave with a mighty leap

The ocean periodically creates a wave after another
It never needs a reminder from any other

Life too has its periodic ups and downs
That is what it is all about, smiles and frowns

Becoming one with the wave is so great
One blinding cloud of foam, nothing to contemplate

Just flow with the ocean and forget what's not done
There is no Land, Sea or any other loved one

It is just our souls merged in a turbulent roar
We cannot enjoy new oceans until we leave the shore

<u>So Near and yet So Far</u>

It was a dark night
Only the moon had the light

One sole star appeared
Behind a cloud it disappeared

It wasn't the brightest
Nor the quickest nor the biggest

But its love was sincere
To it the moon was very dear

The moon could select who it wanted
It had the light and took things for granted

The star saw the moon in a different light
He thought she was divine and always in a flight

He envied the other stars where the moon had changed their tide
He only wanted to be in Love and by her side

Aeons later the moon was alone in her stay
The other stars had left the Milky Way

The sole star had traveled through many a galaxy
It knew itself better and still had only one fantasy

To meet the Moon and pull her by his side
It would be his turn to change the tide

He asked the Moon how her future would be spent
The Moon blushed and in a new galaxy they went

Looking for an Ideal Mate

Life goes by too fast
Too much wind behind the mast

One cannot help but contemplate
What makes up an ideal mate

She would be outgoing like a Westerner
She would be home-loving like a Far Easterner

She would be beautiful like an Indian
She would be passionate like an Italian

In searching for this mystical person if I ever find
Would I be her ideal mate that she has in mind?

Being Alone

Are you happy alone
Fighting life on your own

Do you want a love and support forever
Or wait for the ultimate desire

What do you want tell me
I can be your fantasy

I am what I am and proud
Until you clear up your own cloud

Is it love about which you dream
Or a void to be filled, it seems

Think my dear but think fast
This life is sometimes too short to last

My love has lasted from my reincarnation
I can accept you under any situation

For true love is unconditional
Though life is so educational

I leave you today with your decision
For my dear there are plenty of fish in the ocean

The Flitting Soul

Oh Soul, What do you seek
Think seriously and to me speak

Shelter, money, and food,
For those and other toys
God has been good

Health, looks and clothes
A wholesome life and more
You already have those

Relationship with a mate
Being compassionate to each other
If true that is great

In a pattern we fall
Selecting partner with wrong traits
Not compatible at all

Spending time in a fight
Over pettiness and nonsense
Missing the light

Two people sometimes find
Asserting the ego is important
Happiness controlled by mind

One should love more
Enter the house smilingly
Leave the ego at the door

The soul wants love and more
A loving touch and care
As exciting as a distant shore

Far Apart

*How does one explain the feeling
When the person with whom you are dealing*

*Has a mind of their own and cannot share the heart
The two sometimes remain so far apart*

*You want to love and love
The other wants to be above*

*In love there is no up or down
Sometimes you are serious or sometimes a clown*

*Why does everything have to be black or white
This is a love not war, so are we proving might?*

*Just need a hug and reassurance for the day
It is not just your body I seek for play*

*It is the light from your soul
That makes my empty life whole*

*It is not your money to which I want to link
I thirst for a loving soul form which I can drink*

It is not only your beauty that I am after
It is the tenderness of your soul I want forever

How can one go on smiling with such a storm within
Take the challenge of Life, and if you are happy
you're winnin'

The Weekend

It is a beautiful Saturday
Thoughts of love come my way

The moments are so precious right now
To be shared with a person somewhere somehow

Was life meant to be alone
Or to be together and then be on my own

The wait is painful and maybe it's never late
It's a matter of time to seek your soul mate

It was a beautiful Saturday
The sun sent me warmth my way

My Company Reunion

I received a call late on day
I recognized the voice right away

It was from a dear friend who invited me
For a company get-together unexpectedly

We were having a reunion for my ex-company
It was an occasion for joy and happiness for many

When employed by them, I was overseas many a day
Inspired by a job I thought would stay

I know the reason why I had left the institution
My 6-year old had posed the question

"Dad, is your job your boss?"
The innocent eyes left me at a loss

Shortly after that I changed my job promptly
But my heart goes out to the employees eventually

To be manipulated by people with no foresight
It was sad when they couldn't see the light

Today I am happy my own master
I wish my friends can avoid any disaster

Attachments

We come into the world alone
Our personalities are formed a few short years later

We surround ourselves with our self-created web
We seek the impossible in every field

We want to have the perfect job at our business
No such company or enough time in a day

We want to have the perfect mate
Who is in step with our cycles

We soon realize they have their own cycles
They will continue in the same sequence

One need a close friend to sometimes share
A loving touch and with compassion to care

For such a friend I would give my soul
Would always have my ears, even when I grow old

Blessed are those who find such friends
Even more blessed when that friend becomes a mate

The attachment is not to a person or thing
The soul transcends and goes on living

The best attachment one can have is to Him
The overflowing fountain of Love is always giving

Still we go on wanting and waiting
Instead of only giving love and go on giving

When one realizes then they would be conscious
Of a sweeter and more rewarding life than ever

Love can be a One-way Street

There was no commitment of love on your side
But lovers can fantasize and they want to glide

They want to soar through the air
Away from reality which is a scare

You can continue to love another
But my soul is committed to no other

Being in love is more fun than the thrill of the chase
Love is love, it isn't a chattel or race

We all have to follow our dreams
Even though it pulls us apart at the seams

I wish you luck and I hope you find
Whatever you desire and it gives you peace of mind

Deep down though I hope one day
You'll back on my one-way street and meet half way

When I am in a shell

When I am in a Shell
I feel the world is Hell

I don't care for any person
I feel so empty within

I wonder why I get pain
I only sought love to gain

I search for answers within my soul
My emotions often twirl in a black hole

I often wonder if there is a true soul mate for me
Or is life just a series of a fleeting fantasy

I don't know if it is just fate
Or is it expecting too much from my mate

When my mate and I do well
Surprisingly I'm out of the shell

I am bright and smiling all the way
When I enter people think it's a sunny day

Nobody can ever guess what I've been through
Most don't notice but my true well-wishers do

Just being me

You can get a high from a beautiful day
It's good to forget the world and just play

A stroll on the beach, chase a seagull
Imitate a sea lion's bark whenever there is a lull

I loved being free and letting the ocean cool my feet
Nectar traveled through my body, lessened the heat

I stopped to help children build a castle in the sand
My own castle could never be on land

The castle would be in the clouds far away
Foundation of love and trust, not of rocks and clay

The windows look out to the world for observation
No preconceived grudges in any situation

Wallpaper made of memories of the pleasant events
Unpleasant baggage flushed out of the vents

The bedroom would be a special place to stay
For loving and nurturing at the end of the day

The castle would be for the queen and the kind
Nothing could come between us-nothing unkind!

A day by myself was too short it seems
It was big enough though for all my dreams

Expectations

How do I address the emptiness
Materially wealthy, still not completeness

A flower can sometimes cause an uplift
At times we feel that we are adrift

In a small dinghy in a rough ocean
It is my soul in turbulent emotion

I know what I want
It is not what He grants

To fill one's time with meaningless relations
It is a true waste of sincere intentions

Why not be free as the wind blows
Follow your dreams wherever it goes

True love will come your way
When least expected it will even stay

The Lost Love

It ended too fast
I thought it would last

The day I saw her, I felt there was no other
The only person I wanted to smother

She had the sweetest smile
Could keep me warm for a mile

When I got to know she had a deeper side
She did not only love but she wanted to glide

Suddenly she spread her wings and flew away
I wondered why until today

If I meet her someday
I would have this to say

I realize why she went away
There were differences that were there to stay

But years later maturity and compassion are high on my list
I hope she could hear me in the mist

I would love to pull her away if she was in strife
And once again make her a part of my life

The Oasis

My life was like a desert with blowing sand
Dry, parched I was missing the land

Never knew into which trap I may fall
After being down so much I cannot recall

I saw an oasis in the yonder
Were you a mirage I started to ponder

Then I was touched by your tone
Suddenly I was never going to be alone

For true love can revive a lost soul
Quench my thirst and make me feel whole

The Rough Seas

Can it wash away all the sorrow,
And leave not a worry for tomorrow

The undercurrents I was told were very strong,
My pain too had lasted very long

Shall I dive in and forget
Will it cause me some regret

Will the undercurrents swallow me,
Or will I rise and be free?

Is it parachuting from a plane
Though some may call it insane

One only truly lives by dying,
Believe me I am not lying

I jumped head on into the big one,
I rose from the water to find out I had won

I was cured by all of my fear,
Once again Life was much more dear

What is Peace?

Moving to your center I'm told
Makes you develop and unfold

When no intoxicant can relax you
When no person can understand you

You move inward to your soul
It is only then you can feel the universe in whole

It is a learning process a slow daily shot
Why run, the emotions are so hot

Slice it down a layer at a time
Find out for whom your soul chimes

It may be another soul mate or a higher power
It will be someone from whom love can shower

You start the journey with an open mind
Not knowing what webs you will find

Something familiar that we only have weaved
A concept of Life that we have dreamed

This Life is so short anyway
Why cling to it and worry day after day

There is a purpose why we are here
The day you realize that the rest is clear

What You Mean To Me

You have taught me reality
Before that Life was a fantasy

I thought I could live with my lies
Not realizing why a soul dies

Now I can face the world and stay
Because I know who I am today

You are my inspiration forever
No matter what I endeavor

Don't every be far anymore
My soul forever has been so sore

Come glide with me to our enchanted land
Life can be so much fun hand in hand

Why I write Poems

I never thought I could write
I always believed in the pen and its might

The sword of love left its mark
I bled internally for years in the dark

It was when I confronted a dearly loved one
My heart opened up suddenly and became undone

My wounds opened the feelings and words have poured out
I wanted to live again and to dance and shout

Now that I have started to write I can't seem to stop
The world is so beautiful I never want to get off

The things that have hurt you on the past
Will go on doing so only until you want them to last

Nature has given us such a wonderful grace
Express yourself in God's beautiful given space

Random Emotions

My heart is filled with emotion
I don't know for whom I store this passion

But one thing is for sure it will be for the lucky one
Someone who has been through life and has a zest for fun

I wanted to give and give from the heart
Most people wanted to take and then depart

In my subconscious I wanted some care
I'll give you 50%, can you do 50% of your share?

In my soul, it's only love it desires and chants
No money, no castles and career does it ever want

Just a long hug and a sincere kiss tonight
Makes me all charged up for tomorrow's fight

Sometimes I wonder how some people can live
Without love, emotions can just go through a sieve

I'll find a soul mate who can hold my emotions
Will fill her life with love and her soul with passion

Life was meant to be shared lovingly and never end
I will find that partner before my sun descends

Perception

She said I hurt her
When married, I thought it was forever

She said I kept mentioning her wrongs
It was only to love my soul belongs

I was overflowing with love form within
Getting little reciprocation from another person

Some understanding instead of a glare
Would have quenched my upcoming flare

She had a jewel she wouldn't know
She had interrupted my life's flow

Should I take care of her feelings
When my emotions were no part of her dealing

But we both are too head strong
You don't have to seek the wrong

Or the faults of the other
Or else find another

Then only we can realize what we had
And whether our judgment was good or bad

My Father

I remember him tall and he had his way
A strong breeze took away his soul one day

He lay there cold and lifeless
Leaving me behind tearless

He took great care and a lot of pain
Never did he complain

Gave us the best of education and love
Wanted us to rise above

He though was raised like an orphan
Fought against all odds with great spirit within

He was driven not by the mind but by his heart
That one common gene that will never keep us apart

Today I'm a father and I realize what he would do
Regretting why I argued, even if he wanted the best for you

Family and the Future

I was spending summer happily alone
My family returned home, and I didn't phone

I realized how much they loved me
I was so confused on how life should be

All summer, I was searching for the light
I put forth my best and put all my might

Then I saw your silhouette in the sun
I felt that my life had just begun

I want too much love in Life
Didn't matter if it came from a lover or my wife

Relations are only in the world for show
The soul only follows where love goes

So I live my life waiting for the perfect passion
Never diminishing my love for life or compassion

Who does it beat for?

Today my heart beats very fast
I didn't know how long life would last

Memories of my past flew by my head
I wanted to breathe and stay ahead

My loves, my desires my dreams
Only one short life it seems

Wanting love fulfillment and understanding
Is that asking for too much or demanding

To be happy when your partner is
No matter what the reason, it is bliss

Why does ego ever have to come in the way
It has a place outside my universe, there it should stay

I leave the light on for you every day
I know our paths are destined … on the same way

My Path

I care for many seemingly
Don't want to be emotional deeply

I remember my loved ones everyday
Don't want to be sentimental anyway

I have compassion for all
Passion only for one I can recall

My soul thirst for a drink
A love potion, don't want to think

I am on this path called Life
Without love it is only a strife

<u>Separate Paths</u>

He provided for her every need
She too was a good wife indeed

There was something lacking
It was as if the wall was cracking

The years passed by the kids were grown
They looked back at life at what it had shown

Would they ever do this again to anybody
They both said not over their dead body

Today they are happy again
In separate houses enjoying their domain

The Phases of the Moon

The moon was full tonight
It filled my life so bright

It reminded me of the days with you
When the feelings were so true

The moon was quarter later on
It made me wonder how life had gone

Before I met you I only existed
The moments together I truly lived

The moon was half today
Wonder what changed our ways

The agreements and disagreements would always stay
The pleasant moments together would make them fade away

The moon was dark today
There is hope on the way

For after every a dark night
There is a morning, so bright

The Day Changed

The day was bright and clear
My love for you was so dear

Then a phone call saying he's back changed my life
You really were someone else's wife

I wanted to tear the clouds away
To let sunshine into our lives everyday

I wanted to be so many different things when we were together
I felt we had a lifetime and why rush and bother

But I learnt that life can change instantly
Also one should never take it lightly

I still feel a sense of happiness today
That he is back in your life to stay

I couldn't live being in his shadow
My nature is that I can never follow

I am what I am and so happy today
That I am released, for how long-can't say

The day was bright and clear
I smiled but my soul was filled with tears

The Moon and I

I went a little late for my evening walk
It was almost night and I didn't want to talk

The air was cool and the sky was clear
It was time to think about what was dear

Although we are separated in time and space
We could both look at the moon and share its grace

The moon was a quarter, but worth its weight in gold
It was beautiful and divine and had one solitary star in its hold

It was rather surprising that although it was a lovely summer day
I could just see two heavenly bodies enjoying the Milky Way

I could see the moon blushing and trying to keep a straight face
I imagined the moon becoming full and I saw you on its surface

The star was lonely but not for long
The moon created a storm that was strong

The star moved towards the moon at the speed of light
The moon, too was energized and she became very bright

There was a sweet explosion that lit up the sky
That only left just two happy souls, the Moon and I

Why-o-Why

Why can't it be
That two persons never see

The joy of seeing the Light
Is always in their might

Rather than see the love in the Eyes
They are drowned in the shouts and cries

Just stop, turn and listen,
Do not fly by and hasten

It is more rewarding to give than to receive,
It is more satisfying to be honest than to deceive

A marriage based only on relatives, materialism and sex
In those cases, life is just a hex

It is the love in the soul that was to be shared
By someone who really cared

The Waves of Life will beat upon people with such ferocity,
It is the strong bond that will fight back with tenacity

The bond needs to be nurtured
Without Love it will be punctured

Do what you can to see eye to eye
Otherwise that relation is destined to die

Life

I had a life before you came my way
I thought it was only day to day

You showed me how I could be much better
You wanted to push me although I was a go-getter

Now that I have changed for the better today
Our paths are too far away

I had a life before you came
To spend it without you is a shame

The Moon can change the tide

The Moon was bright on an evening of a summer day
Over the yonder an eagle searching for a prey

Always hungry and looking to satisfy its need
So was my soul looking for the impossible indeed

Below the moon ran two parallel strips of cloud like darts
Just like two hungry souls close in their lives yet so apart

They would meet again in another time and space, in happiness
Not having any prior memories of society and peoples' pettiness

The moon would still be there to see them side by side
As it is the moon's duty to change the tides

Time will Tell

The time together wasn't' long
The bond created was very strong

I saw myself clearly with you
I realized what I really wanted to do

I nurtured you the way I would like to be
With you by my side my soul was so happy

Our dream ended abruptly when we had to part
We may be away but always close to the heart

For what we shared, people will never in a lifetime
Pleasant memories will carry me the rest of my time

In the future we will meet again
The love we shared will reduce any pain

A Ray of Hope

The winter days came to an end
The clouds were heavy and started to descend

To fill the thirsty earth that was dry
Just like my life before was like a barren sky

This was the winter of being discovered
Realizing what I am, my emotions uncovered

Beside you we went through valleys and peaks
I knew that in my heart what I wanted to seek

Alas one cannot control the partner's heart's desires
What is deep down, what lights the fire

We parted in spring as our worlds were apart
So much love we shared deep in our heart

In another time after your roller-coaster ride
We may re-kindle our relation and live side by side

I look at the sun on a cloudy day
I always say a ray of hope coming my way

To Know Me

Don't ask me about the Past
There's not enough time for my story to last

I know you have a past too
It's deeper than the oceans blue

Just love me for what I am
Walk along the ocean hold my hand

Let the waves cleanse not only our feet but our hearts
Remove all the pain and sorrow that keeps people apart

Walk by my side, not ahead or behind
I want us equal in both body and mind

Make no promises, for who has seen tomorrow
Just be by each other's side in happiness and sorrow

Just look ahead together in the distant way
Thank God that we have each other, every single day

A Wonderful Life

With every breath I take today
I am amazed at what Life has to say

It is a world of growth and wonderment
Being a healthy human is His best accomplishment

We have close ones as near as we choose to keep
Sometimes relationships can hurt when too deep

It is a world of giving and love
A light coming from above

We often are in the dark and miss the light
Until we look inward and stop doubting His might

No person or relationship is so great
Whose loss cannot be overcome, that is Fate

When one feels they are drowning in a rough sea
They have to stop struggling and let it be

Once that happens you are lifted by Nature's flow
Despite any loss, His Love will make you glow

Lost in the Mist

On the side of the mountain my house lay
I wanted to reach the top on a cloudy day

At the crack of dawn it was cool and clear
I left the ground and all that was dear

The climb was hard and it was steep
My feelings were strong and my pain was deep

I was overflowing with love and passion within
Maybe, selfishly, expecting reciprocation from the right person

I put the thoughts aside and reached halfway
From that height the possessions and desires seemed small and faraway

After that a fog sank in
Was I in earth or in heaven

I could no longer see my house or the people within
I had no other desire but to go on climbin'

I saw a bright light break through the fog from the heavens above
It was His way of telling me how wonderful it was just to love

There was a delicate balance between giving up the world and moving to the light
Although I stood empty I was filled with love and with no one in sight

I realized I could give Him love and it could only bring me joy
It was the only relationship so unselfish that we could both enjoy

I cleared my thoughts at the top of the peak
I felt He had told me a lot, although I didn't hear him speak

I felt this was the beginning and definitely not the end
I could reach newer heights as I started to descend

My Mate

We got married young and I brought her to a foreign land
We were like children lost in a sea of sand

We went through the trials of Life
Getting possessions and that was quite a strife

The most beautiful part was the kids and the joys
They were born out of love and were both girls not boys

She was a pillar of strength and took care of kids while I earned the bread
I sometimes thank God for her, otherwise I couldn't see ahead

Years later we've both grown up and think how quickly life has gone by
I often wonder if I had another mate and I'm sure she does too, how would the time fly

There were years I wasn't perfect stressed by financial woes
She had too her times when she wanted her own way and egos

After years of togetherness I awoke with a chill
And asked do I want the rest of my life going uphill

Life was meant to be give and take
Being good at only one, does not a couple make

A ship of marriage built of love and respect can last
Can move icebergs, the faith is like wind to a mast

Navigating a ship is a challenge for the captain and his mate
Every day we are stressed by Life and sometimes by Fate

Today, I live my life patiently, hope that we'll be a team
So we see each other not only in the day but also lovingly in our dreams

Life in Stages

I simply cannot end this song
I know Life isn't very long

We come here for a short stay
Even the greatest have to leave one day

The first stage we are loved and nurtured
By our dear ones and we become cultured

The second stage off to college we go
To learn a lot, least our ignorance we show

The third stage we are wrapped with our career and marriage
And make sure we pay for the house and carriage

The fourth stage our children become grown
We want to give them better than what we've ever known

The fifth stage is the empty nest
This is time to be spiritual and take rest

The sixth stage we look back and approach the end
We want to stretch every day longer and watch the sun descend

Life is six short stages
Although it may seem like ages

Life can be lead in a special way
When you want to do a good deed do it today

If you want to do a bad deed today
Postpone and think about for at least a day

This is the best way of being happy today and tomorrow
Fill your life with laughter and leave no room for sorrow

The Fork on the Road

To climb the hill there were many a trail
One could select the easy way or hold a rail

I selected a path that was steep
For my feelings were too deep

The mind was heavy but gentle was my pace
For the steps I take I can never retrace

On reaching a fork about half way
My mind was racing with thoughts today

On one side I had my past
On the other side a future I wanted to last

I was in the present thinking
A clear day, intoxication without drinking

Half my life like the climb was over
At this point the patterns are set forever

My past had people I was responsible for
But in Life there to be love respect and more

I had to think about culture and tradition
I also had to think about my soul and not convention

I selected the unknown path for the future that day
Knowing I would meet my soul mate on the way

The Hike to the Top

It was a bright and perfect summer day
The mountain was beckoning me to come its way

I packed my water in my backpack
You don't need much more than a light snack

The hike was long and the air was pure
Refreshing my mind and it was the perfect cure

Memories of love, relations and work came by
I tossed them and could barely see them from the sky

I was going to a newer height and didn't want to be late
I wasn't going to get there with all the emotional weight

The summit was beautiful and calm
I looked the skies and stretched out my palm

I asked for His Blessing to make the world a beautiful place
I felt He smiled and told us to enjoy every moment and not treat Life as a race

Being Free

I want to glide
Never take any sides

Go to places unknown
Live in laughter no moans

See the children smiling
Learn about life without trying

Not go into work for pay
The world is my office everyday

My home is where I find love
It can be in the open under the skies above

The only cover that warms my soul when I sleep
That I was loved by someone who feelings were deep

The Half Moon

The moon was half today
Just like my life on many a day

I have a bright side wherever I go
But the other side no one will ever know

To be smiling in life one must also cry
To know what rain is, one must be dry

To be complete in love, one must also be alone
To know what happiness is, you must sorrow and moan

To be one with Him, one must also know evil
To go to the righteous path, you will have to kill your own devil

I am but human and have done deeds I regret
I still believe I am blessed and I should never forget

A New Beginning

Why does a heart feel so empty
Like a dinghy in a rough sea

The memory of your sweet smile
Helps me paddle every mile

To an undiscovered land far away
Waiting for an adventurer to come and stay

There are no long unending corridors of walls
Have been in my imaginations causing me to stall

There are no flapping doors of emotions that open and shut
Just fresh breeze through four sides of a hut

There is just fresh thoughts in the air everyday
Only time to discover what is life and love in every way

I will build my castle for my soul mate and change her tide
Come swim to me, we'll never leave each other's side

Chapter 2

My love, my life has once again begun
The joy of breathing, seeing the light of sun

You came again into my life so graciously
Each moment was spent so preciously

Under the sweet smile and care
The fears you will never share

I thought know why you did what you did
The reasoning of your mind was never hid

The only pain I bear today
Will be the memories of yesterday

For tomorrow you will be in a different land
I will be parched again with an outstretched hand

You can never be too far away
For life was not meant to be that way

After the fog lifts and the reasons are apparent
Then you will see that all relations are transparent

I hope I can hold my breath that long
I pray that love can keep me strong

For you are the purest goddess of love
Wherever you are my little white dove

What will the future hold?

I have spent a long time thinking
Sometimes even longer drinking

Wondering what life was about
Marriage, family and being in and out

The biggest scare is that when you give without thinking
The world will only suck you and soon you will be sinking

Devoid of your peace of mind and even money
So don't feel you've hit the bottom honey

The wise allow themselves to be cheated
They themselves would never cheat, the purpose would be defeated

If one allows him to be cheated consciously
They have reached a different height knowingly

But I am only human and feel robbed of my emotions
I thought by giving would reduce the perturbation

I gave and gave and my well ran dry
My soul was so sad, nobody could hear my cry

Yet outwardly I always feel the future is bright
With His smile, I can always feel the light

The Birthday by the Sea

Is there a better way to turn forty
Than by the Indian Ocean and Arabian Sea

The majestic waves beat upon the shore,
The land tells the ocean I want you more and more

The Ocean is mighty and deep
Within its center, many secrets it keeps

The land is dry and full of holes
The ocean fills life into the thirsty souls

I stood by the shore waiting for my wave to appear,
I waited to be embraced and finally disappear

<u>Love and Being in Love</u>

*She didn't know
Why she would glow*

*She loved someone
He knew he had won*

*She didn't know about being in love
Would put them both above*

*And lead a far happier life
than any man and wife*

*love doesn't care for a relation
It just creates an elevation*

*To lighten one from the day to day
To carry our spirits far away*

*Someday she would know the difference
When her unlocked mind can draw an inference*

*By that day I will be far away
A free spirit has only moments to stay*

Lovers are Givers

What is this mystical word
The unspoken so it is never heard

It fills the world with light
It makes one's days so bright

It is the stretching of a child's reach
Towards his mum on a rough beach

It is two lovers holding hands in the dark
Their eyes light the air with a spark

It is a brother saying farewell to his sister
Knowing his fondest thoughts are always with her

Why does it sometimes cause so much pain
Can someone every try to explain

It has a special place in one's heart for a short stay
It is cannot be experienced unless you give it away

Do not be scared to hold back and share
Life is really fun only when you care

Some people think of it as just a play
Their acting will make them lonely some day

There is no winner or loser in a relationship indeed
True lovers are givers and in Life they will succeed

Divali-The Indian New Year

The Festival of Lights, the Indian New Year
Time to forget the past, hug who is dear

We are involved with other things
Enjoy every pleasure that life brings

We are far apart only in space
The souls are together in one place

It is so special, the Divali night
There is no need for any light

Other than the joyous glow from your eyes
That sends me a warm feeling across the skies

Release

We hurt each other
Shouldn't we love another

Long years together sometimes
Makes the heart stop its chimes

We need to rewind the keys
And speed to where the heart flees

No thoughts for friends or family
Why torture ourselves for society

I have no desire to hurt you
You have the same feeling too

Why should one suffer in this life so short
We can always start life anew somewhat

Release me and let me follow
all my dreams, let it bring joy or sorrow

I do the same for you today
Wishing that happiness may forever stay

Teachers

The years at school flew by
Sometimes we laughed and sometimes we sighed

Our teachers gave us special attention and care
Making us logical and also teaching us to share

Geography taught us of lands on a distant shore
A whole wide world that we would explore

Spending time on teaching us languages and history
Explaining why things tick and removing the mystery

Science and Mathematics are sometimes a chore
They made it interesting, making us curious even more

The PE teacher was tough, the Music teacher was kind
So they tuned not only the body but also the mind

I have more respect for teachers not what I'm a father
They could have picked any profession but they'd rather

Spend time imparting knowledge and themselves
And if we have succeeded it is not by ourselves

A great part of the equation
Was how the teachers laid our foundation

I would pick new relatives, if I lived my life again
The school and teachers I would keep the same

My daughter became a Teenager

She was just a baby in my arms yesterday
Today, suddenly is her thirteenth birthday

She has grown up so beautiful and slender
I wish that she always remains sweet and tender

I remember pushing her in the swing
She was so small and she said sweet nothings

She was alone until she was four
Then she got another sister to adore

She wanted to play with her from the day she was arrived
Little did she know that it takes a while, until then she would have to be deprived

Her name meant music and that made her alive
She danced on the stage from the time she was five

She always supported her mum, no matter what the situation
For a little child she only got my admiration

She entered school and became a part of the flow
She studied when she had to and her grades were so-so

She had a lot of potential if only she knew it at all
If she put her mind to anything the world would be at her beck and call

The years ahead will be like walking on the fresh snow
You must tread carefully as your footsteps will show

A friend told her, it is better to toil for another ten years and enjoy the rest of your life
Then to fool around for ten, and make the rest just an unending strife

I can only hope the best for my little princess everyday
From the path of truth and righteousness, may she never sway

A New Baby in the family

A beautiful message awaited me on the phone
My brother and his wife would no longer be alone

They had a beautiful bonnie baby and she looked great
She looks like the mum, no she looks like the dad, and has a lovely face

They had been married for long
Their first baby would only make them strong

For now it wasn't just life living for two
They are now a family and have lots to do

The cute eyes, the bouncing head, the pretty nose
Soon she would decide where the family goes

My heart was filled with blessings from within
I sent them the message in a breeze across the ocean

Loving Daughters

Why do little girls grow up so fast
We want their childhood to last

From their parents they receive so much love
Then one day they fly away like a dove

They build their nest with a new person
Hoping they will receive all the lovin'

It is a challenge when one compares in the mind
Especially when you have left all the loved ones behind

To change and adapt to a new life
By being in a new house, someone's wife

Early years of marriage can be a trial and tribulation
Only love and compromise can resolve the situation

Life is a Roller-coaster

I thought we were doing fine
But my fears were not left behind

She felt deeply I had hurt her
I hadn't a clue what did I do whenever

When she came back to me I was filled with love
I wanted to be so close and make us rise above

We were below sea level now and I felt so low
I tried to fill my body with spirits and let my smile show

The liquor had no effect as my soul was sad
No intoxicant could make it glad

When a couple can't understand each other it's a shame
We have no one but ourselves to blame

By keeping emotions within and worrying about petty things
We lose control of our happiness and only sorrow it brings

I wanted a relationship where we could sing, dance and rejoice

However in this life I wonder if I have a choice

To break up one's marriage is like dropping a shoe
It's how one salvages a relationship is more challenging to do

I want to go on a mountain and shout aloud
I want to be far away from the madding crowd

I want a life of harmony and give each other space
If she only knew how highly I regarded her in her place

Maybe it's only a cycle and she will change no doubt
Meanwhile, I'm on the Roller-coaster and it's turning me inside-out

The moment is now

It is all right to be soft and weak
One great person said "Blessed are the meek"

The earth would be inherited by those
It would not go to the strong even though they destroyed the foes

When one is born they are soft and tender
No matter what the race or gender

When one dies one is rigid and hard and unmoving
A few years on this planet caused so much transforming

A person should always be like a rose, beautiful and gentle
Radiate happiness wherever you go, and even when you are still

Most people with egos relate more to a rock
Relationships based on money, property and stock

They have become rigid and hard before their time
Being dead before dying was certainly a crime

A child's actions are worth observing

Love and anger occur in moments but it is only fleeting

Our children can teach us like any sage
For their souls and visions are unblemished at that age

We have to live for the present moment and not the past
A simple formula that can make a gentle life last

Soul Mates

Who am I to you?
Our souls are somehow connected too

We have a special relation
That raises my spirit's elevation

Why do you stay so far
My thirst cannot be quenched by any bar

Whenever I speak to you
My soul loses all its blue

I feel energized again
I forget all the pain

When I inhale you are in my breath
You will be my soul mate even after my death

<u>What do you want?</u>

*Can one be truly alone every day
You may have company who will never stay*

*Is it companionship that you desire
Does it satisfy the burning desire*

*To fulfill the intellectual, physical and emotional need
Is that the goal of life indeed?*

*Or is it being in the flow of love
Effortless, coming only from above*

*When the light from a soul touches you
The so called need will cause no more blue*

*For with love you will glow
The only thing that a happy rose can show*

What you mean to me

My Life, my precious my dear
With you by my side I have no fear

You are the epitome of womanhood
A fountain of youth a drink for eternal manhood

A teacher, a disciple, a listener
A treasure, a liability, a speaker

The entire world on the side of the scale
I would choose you on the other side, no tale

For with you I could build all my dreams
And nurture and give you a real life it will seem

You are far away today I know
But I will wait for the date you glow

Experiencing of how life was meant to be
And enjoying every moment before it flees

Looking Inward

The mist was heavy
The road looked murky

I moved slowly in the dark
I had to move forward I couldn't park

I looked on either side
Other were in a very slow stride

All searching for a light
All intelligent and not so bright

I didn't want to move ahead
I took a breath and looked inwards instead

Suddenly the darkness lifted
Mystically the mist had shifted

I could see my own image clear again
I realized that there was no more pain

What is a Relationship

What is a relationship?
Can one jump the ship?

When the oceans get rough
And the reasoning is tough

When there are children with innocent eyes
Whose thoughts are clear as the skies

They can't understand the rift
They don't know why a parents adrift

The parent is in his own world of emotion
Wanting to be at peace no commotion

She wonders want went wrong
"He's in a transition, won't be long"

They may have at some time being ideal for each other
Today if not for the kids, they could not be bothered

Resilience

From far the ocean looked very still
I was in a plane over the hill

When I looked further the waves broke at the shore
Telling the land do you want more

The beach was still and unchanging
Despite their creator's waves and their beating

It was a balance of nature
That life was a strange mixture

Of elements that coexist after centuries of abuse
We are mortals for a short time, we must be gentle
with our use

A Wish

*May the sun shine on your back
So that you're on the go never slack*

*May you travel to places far away
Only to return home happily one day*

*May you be less upset at little things
Life is easier if you laugh than let it sting*

*When you look down the years ahead
The future is bright keep a clear head*

*And down the line we'll meet if you care
We'll reminisce the time we shared*

To have or have not

Why did I give up what I had
Only because I thought I was sad

To leave the comfort of my house
The sincerity of a spouse

I took off to chase my childhood dream
For a person who could make it seem

That I was a king once again
To forgot in life there is pain

The time with her was spent so quickly
The memories will be in my heart deeply

Falling in love elevated my heart
Until the day we had to part

I went back to my sincere spouse
Feeling inside like a louse

Today I look back at what I did
A lesson for which I am glad

I realized a few rash moments of love
Can derail what I have received from above

She's going back

It was another call, and it was early in the day
She was going back to ex and he was going to stay

I laughed and was happy for her on the phone
But I missed a few heartbeats when I was alone

She was a lovely flower
Who only knew love to shower

He had his own life
And decided occasionally that she was his wife

I walked along the beach later that day
Wondering about Life and watching the children play

I watched the pelicans dive and catch something with a fin
I felt as if my soul been scooped out my skin

My love was too deep
But she wasn't mine to keep

If we were destined to meet again, we would in a certain time and place
In the meantime I will enjoy Nature and Life that have so much grace

At the end of the day a certain peace came over me
My true love was happy and my soul was set free

Farewell Rose

The Rose came into my life today
It was a short though beautiful stay

She was on to her new life with the gardener
I was happy though as an observer

She had stories of love and her times
Each precious moment my heart would chime

She touched my soul in so many ways
Her words like music caused me to sway

Underlying all the things she would tell
A scared soul in a child would dwell

A soul I wanted to nourish forever
The more I loved the more I'd confuse her

I should have held back my love
That wouldn't be right though my dove

For I don't know when I will see you again
When I emerge from my darkness, come to your lane

I don't know how my life passed by before her
Soon she would fly, loneliness would replace her

I wish her happiness forever and more
May she smile and safely reach her shore

www.ingramcontent.com/pod-product-compliance
Lightning Source LLC
Chambersburg PA
CBHW061455040426
42450CB00007B/1368